ISBN: 9798864788394

Website: www.jdalearning.com

Email: jdalearning@gmail.com

Youtube Educational Videos: www.youtube.com/c/JadyAlvarez

Instagram: www.instagram.com/jadyahomeschool

Alphabet Manuscript

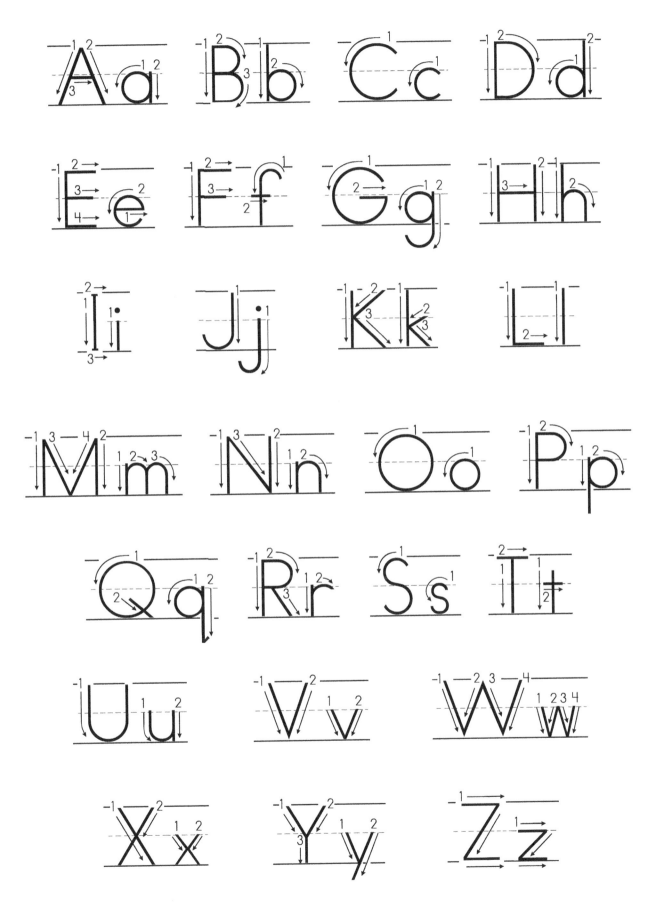

Letter Writing

A a _____

B b _____

C c _____

D d _____

E e _____

Letter Writing

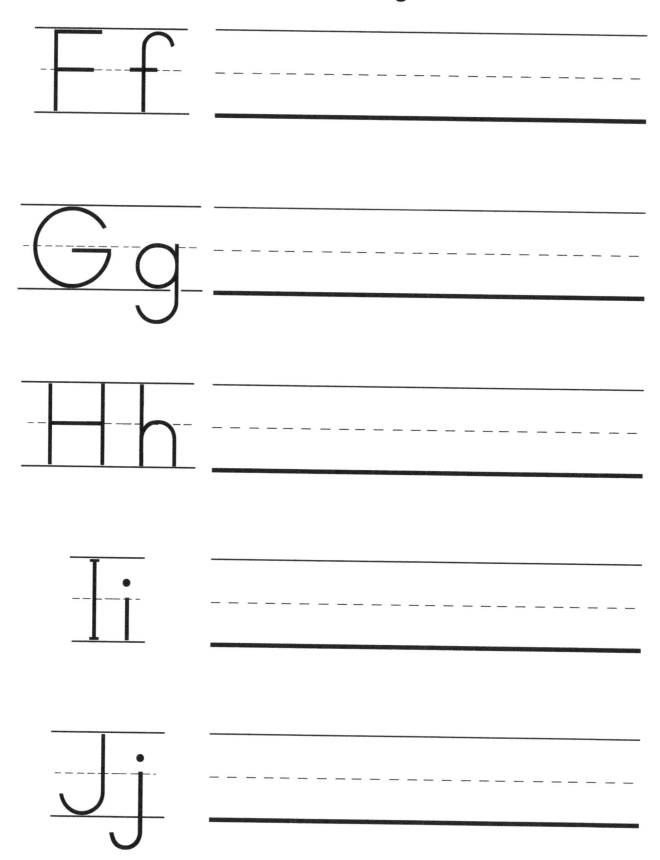

Letter Writing

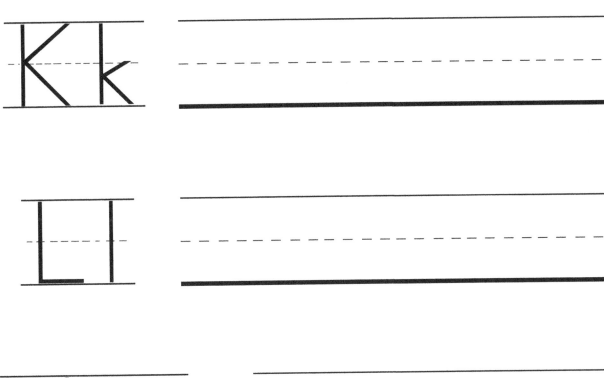

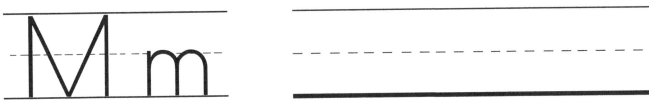

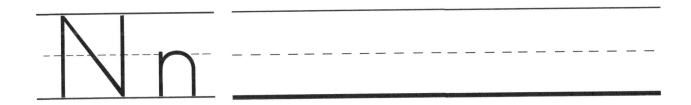

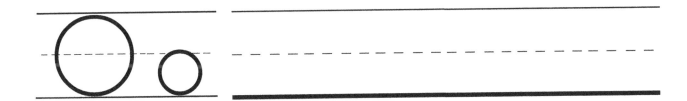

Letter Writing

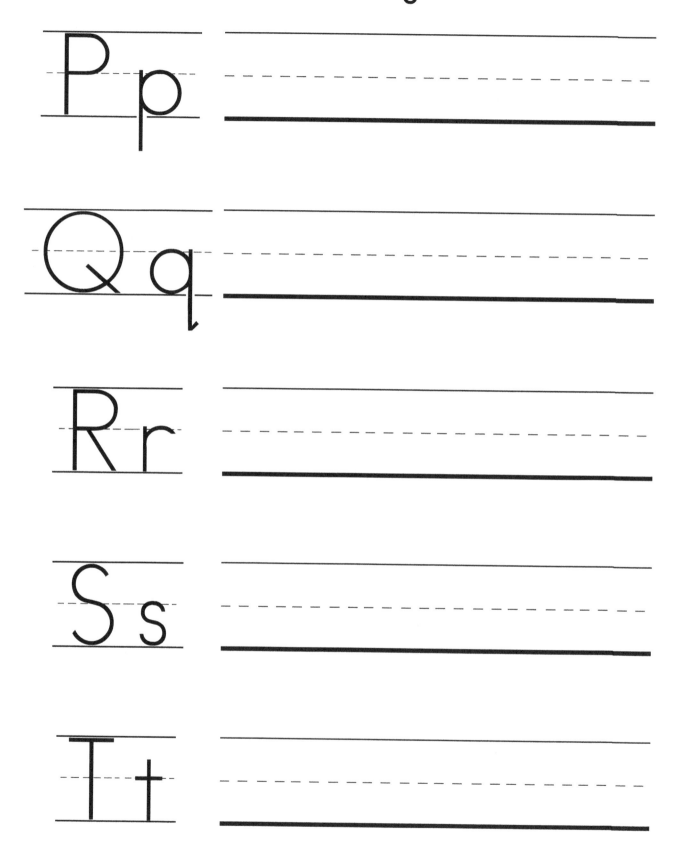

Letter Writing

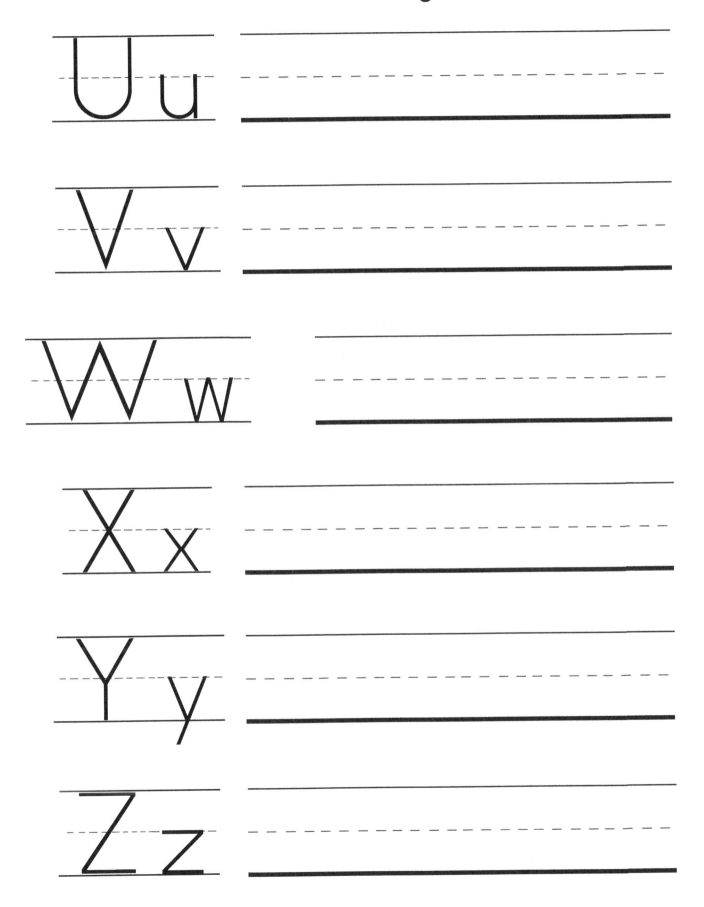

at

bat

cat

hat

mat

sat

en

den

hen

men

pen

ten

ig

big

dig

fig

pig

wig

ot

cot

dot

hot

pot

rot

ug

bug

dug

hug

mug

rug

an

can

fan

man

ran

van

et

jet

net

pet

vet

wet

ip

dip

hip

lip

rip

zip

og

cog

dog

fog

hog

log

un

bun

fun

nun

run

sun

ag

bag

nag

rag

tag

wag

ed

bed

fed

led

red

wed

in

bin

fin

pin

tin

win

ub

cub

hub

rub

sub

tub

ab

cab

dab

jab

nab

tab

id

bid

hid

kid

lid

rid

ob

cob

job

mob

rob

sob

um

bum

gum

hum

rum

sum

ad

bad

dad

had

mad

sad

it

bit

hit

kit

pit

sit

op

cop

hop

mop

pop

top

ap

cap

lap

map

tap

zap

ut

but

cut

gut

nut

rut

Sound out and write the word for every picture.

at

Sound out and write the word for every picture.

en

Sound out and write the word for every picture.

pig wig dig jig big

Sound out and write the word for every picture.

Sound out and write the word for every picture.

bug hug mug rug jug

Sound out and write the word for every picture.

an

can fan ran van man

Sound out and write the word for every picture.

Sound out and write the word for every picture.

og

log hog dog jog fog

Sound out and write the word for every picture.

un

bun sun run nun fun

Sound out and write the word for every picture.

bag rag wag tag flag

Sound out and write the word for every picture.

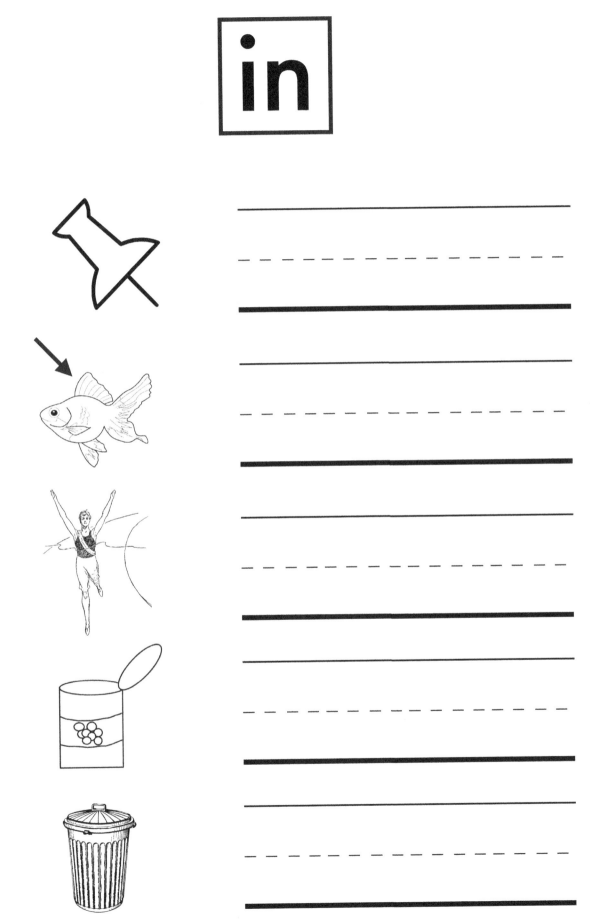

pin fin win tin bin

Sound out and write the word for every picture.

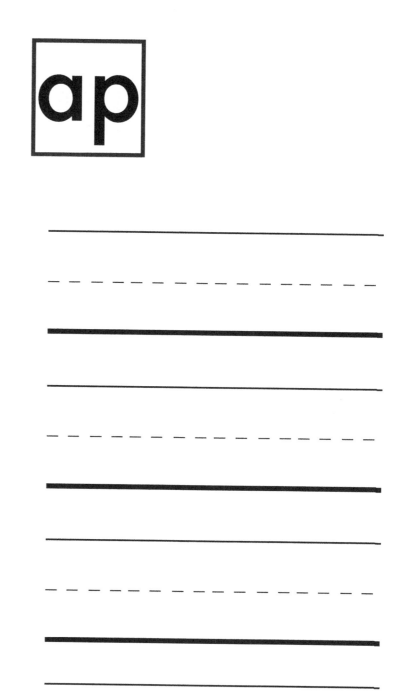

nap cap clap tap lap

Sound out and write the word for every picture.

cut nut gut hut shut

Sound out and write the word for every picture.

mop pop cop stop hop

Sound out and write the word for every picture.

bed fed sled wed led

Copy the sentence.

Pat sat on a mat.

Copy the sentence.

The cat has a hat.

Copy the sentence.

The bug is
under the
rug.

Copy the sentence.

The pig has a wig.

Copy the sentence.

The dog
jumped over
the frog.

Copy the sentence.

Ben has a
pen.

Copy the sentence.

Gus got on the bus.

Copy the sentence.

The net got wet.

_____

- - - - - - - - - - - - - -

═══════════════════════

_____

- - - - - - - - - - - - - -

═══════════════════════

_____

- - - - - - - - - - - - - -

═══════════════════════

Copy the sentence.

Sam had fun in the sun.

Copy the sentence.

Jan ran into the van.

Copy the sentence.

The man got
a tan.

_____

- - - - - - - - - - - - - - -

═══════════════════════

_____

- - - - - - - - - - - - - - -

═══════════════════════

_____

- - - - - - - - - - - - - - -

═══════════════════════

Copy the sentence.

Mom's pot is
hot.

Copy the sentence.

The sub was in the tub.

Copy the sentence.

The lad was sad.

Copy the sentence.

The hen went
into the den.

Dictation Sentences

Read these sentences to the student and have them write one sentence a day. Have the child use phonics to sound out the words and write them as best as they can. When they are done have the child draw a picture.

1) The dog ran.
2) A pig is pink.
3) Mat sat on the mat.
4) The hen is red.
5) The sun is hot.
6) The bug is big.
7) The cat has a hat.
8) The jet went fast.
9) Mom has a wig.
10) Jan got wet.
11) The fox is red.
12) Dad has a van.
13) Dan has a mug.
14) Pat had a nap.
15) Mat hid in the hut.

Listen to the sentence, write it, and draw a picture.

1

Listen to the sentence, write it, and draw a picture.

2

Listen to the sentence, write it, and draw a picture.

3

Listen to the sentence, write it, and draw a picture.

4

Listen to the sentence, write it, and draw a picture.

5

Listen to the sentence, write it, and draw a picture.

6

Listen to the sentence, write it, and draw a picture.

7

Listen to the sentence, write it, and draw a picture.

8

Listen to the sentence, write it, and draw a picture.

9

Listen to the sentence, write it, and draw a picture.

10

Listen to the sentence, write it, and draw a picture.

11

Listen to the sentence, write it, and draw a picture.

12

Listen to the sentence, write it, and draw a picture.

13

Listen to the sentence, write it, and draw a picture.

14

Listen to the sentence, write it, and draw a picture.

15

Made in the USA
Columbia, SC
22 October 2024